LEVEL **2A**

PIANO
Adventures® *Arranged by Nancy and Randall Faber*
A BASIC PIANO METHOD

CONTENTS

1st and 2nd endings

| 1. | 2. |

Play the 1st ending and take the repeat.
Then play the 2nd ending, skipping over
the 1st ending.

(Meet) The Flintstones

Words and Music by
Joseph Barbera, William Hanna,
and Hoyt Curtin

Teacher Duet: (Student plays 1 octave higher)

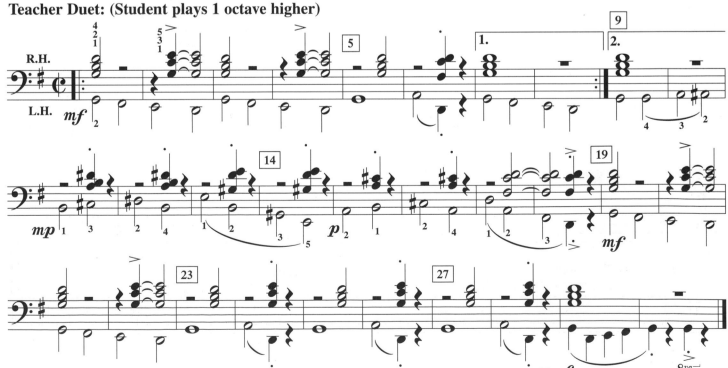

FF1258

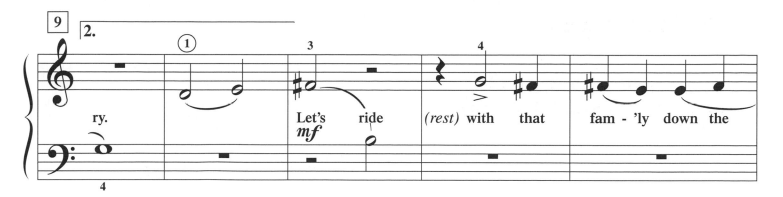

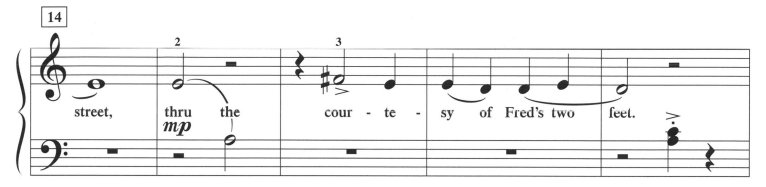

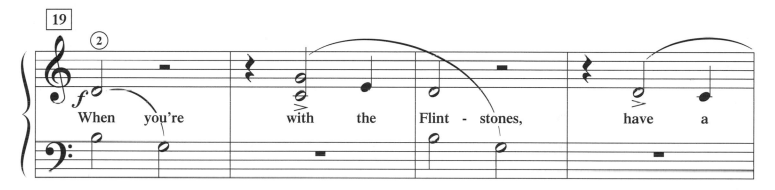

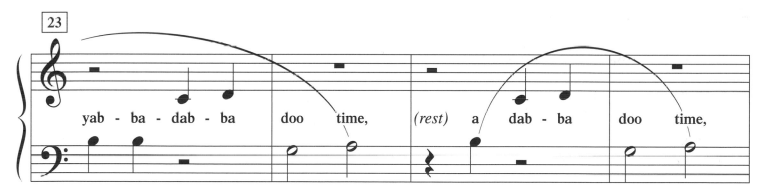

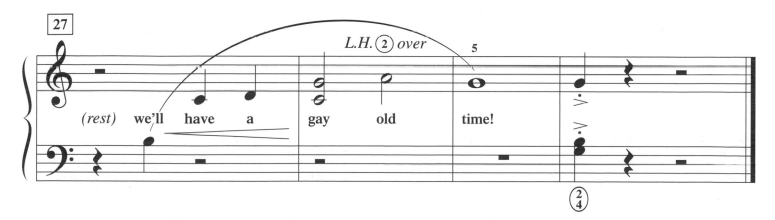

DISCOVERY Write a ✔ above each measure with this rhythm.
Hint: It occurs 6 times.

Stone-Age Theory

(Meet) The Flintstones

Words and Music by
Joseph Barbera, William Hanna,
and Hoyt Curtin

Complete the information above the measures
to learn more about *The Flintstones*.

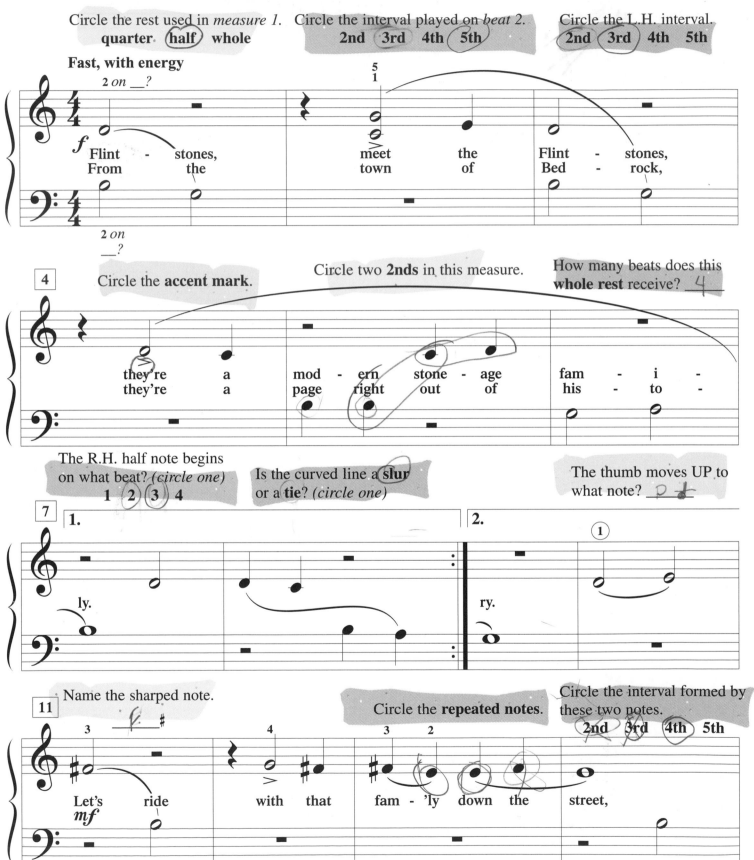

FF1258

8th Notes

♪♪ = ♩

Two eighth notes equal one quarter note.

Theme from *FREE WILLY*

Will You Be There

Written and Composed by
Michael Jackson

Moderately

1 *on* __?

mp Hold me,
mf Hold me,

(1 - 2) lay your head
love me and

low - ly,
feed me,

1 *on* __?
5 *on* __?

(1 - 2) soft - ly then
kiss me and

bold - ly
free me,

car - ry me
I will feel

there. _____
blessed. _____

rit.

Teacher Duet: (Student plays 1 octave higher)

R.H.

L.H.

p-mp on repeat

rit.

FF1258

Musical Whales

Add up the **total number of beats** on each whale.
Then draw a connecting line to the diver with the correct answer.

Extra Credit: Your teacher may ask you to do the following:

1. Write the correct *time signature* before each rhythm.
2. Write the *correct beats* under each rhythm (1 + 2 + 3 + , etc.)
3. Clap (or tap) each rhythm while counting aloud.

The Natural ♮

A natural cancels a sharp or a flat.
A natural is always a white key.

Merrily We Roll Along
from *LOONEY TUNES*

Words and Music by
Eddie Cantor, Charlie Tobias,
and Murray Mencher

Teacher Duet: (Student plays 1 octave higher)

FF1258

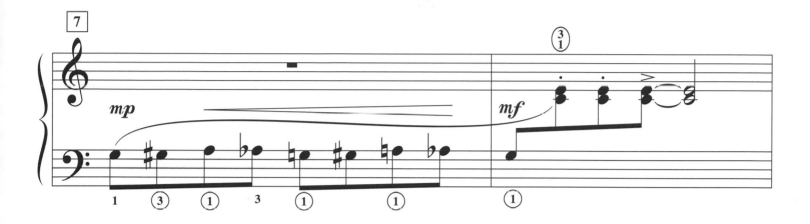

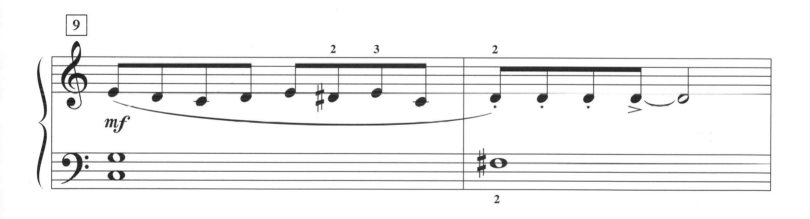

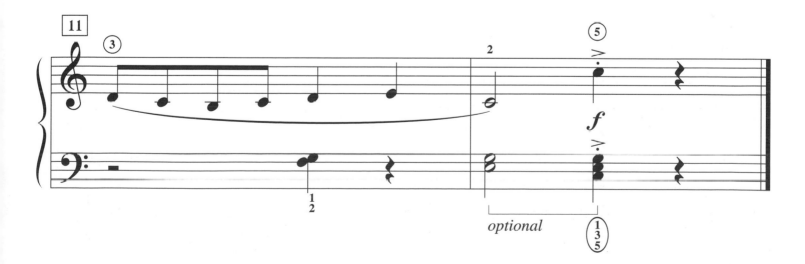

DISCOVERY Where does the melody in *measures 1-2* appear transposed
down a whole step? *measures* _____ and _____

. . . Merrily We Name Our Notes

Merrily We Roll Along

Words and Music by
Eddie Cantor, Charlie Tobias,
and Murray Mencher

Name the notes "in the waves"
as these rowers merrily roll along.
Hint: Be sure to include the #, ♭, or ♮.

R.H. — Ex. E D C D E #D E C

R.H. — D C B C D #C D B

L.H. — G #G A ♭A ♮G #G ♮A ♭A

FF1258

Extra Credit: Your teacher may point to any example
and ask you to play it on the keyboard.

Tiger Rag
(Hold That Tiger)

Lyric by
Harry DeCosta

Music by
Original Dixieland Jazz Band

FF1258

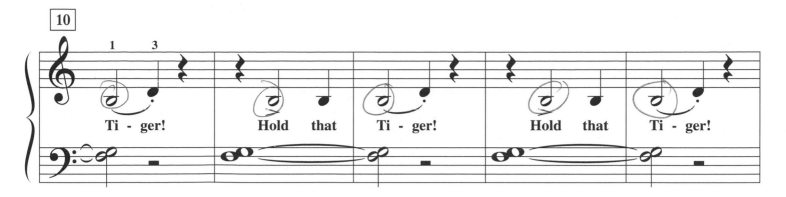

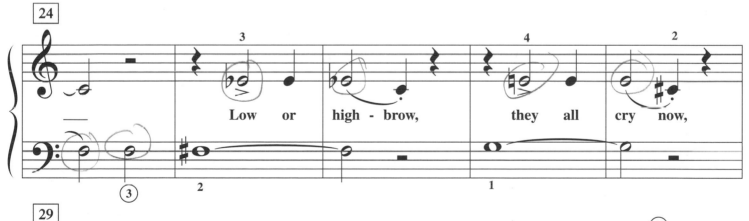

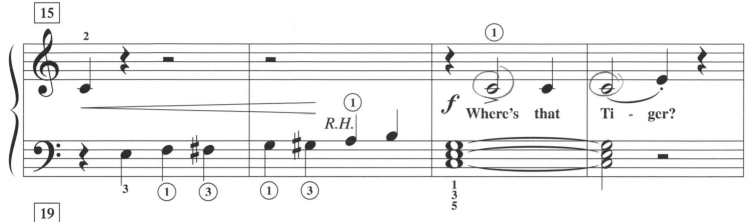

DISCOVERY This two-measure pattern occurs 11 times.
Draw a ✔ at the beginning of each pattern in your music.

Tiger Party

I and V7 Chords in C Position

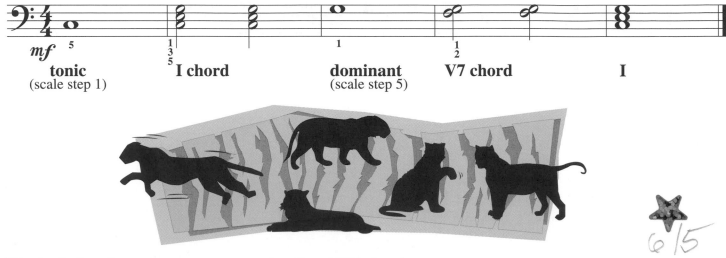

mf 5

tonic
(scale step 1)

I chord

dominant
(scale step 5)

V7 chord

I

Blocked chords are just one way to play **I** and **V7** chords.

Practice each example to discover new ways to play I and V7 chords.
Hint: First practice the L.H. alone, until the chord pattern is easy.

Tiger Rag
(Hold That Tiger)

Music by
Original Dixieland Jazz Band

Lyric by
Harry DeCosta

"Two Paw Jump"

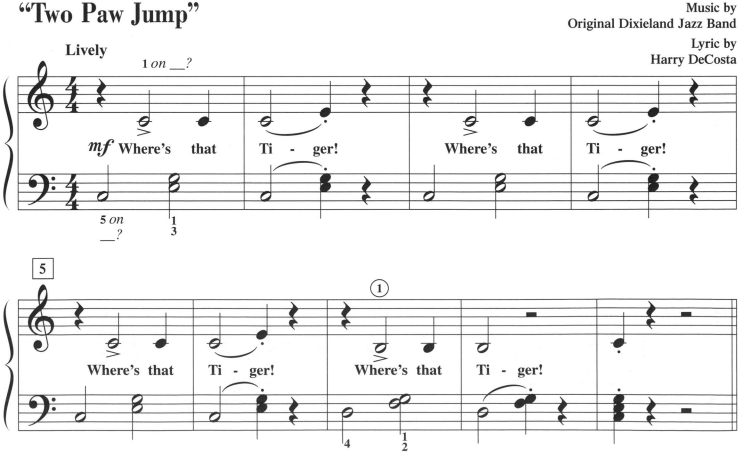

Lively

mf Where's   that   Ti - ger!   Where's   that   Ti - ger!

Where's that   Ti - ger!   Where's   that   Ti - ger!

FF1258

"Four Paw Strut"

Lively

mf Where's that Ti - ger! Where's that Ti - ger!

5

Where's that Ti - ger! Where's that Ti - ger!

"Tiger Tail Twirl"

Lively

mf Where's that Ti - ger! Where's that Ti - ger!

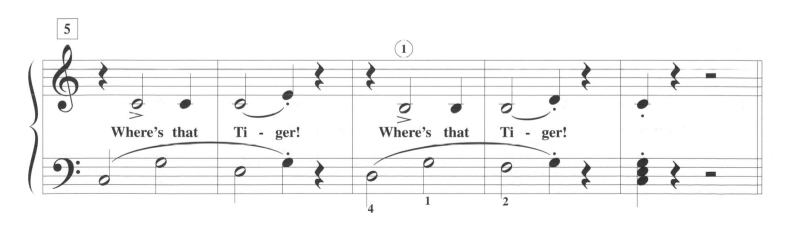

5

Where's that Ti - ger! Where's that Ti - ger!

If I Were a Rich Man

from FIDDLER ON THE ROOF

Lyrics by Sheldon Harnick

Music by Jerry Bock

Lyrics:

If I were a rich man, Dai - dle, dee - dle, dai - dle, dig - guh, dig - guh, dee - dle, dai - dle, dum.

All day long I'd bid - dy, bid - dy bum,

Teacher Duet: (Student plays 1 octave higher)

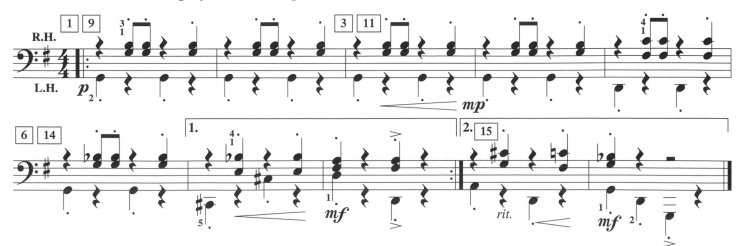

FF1258

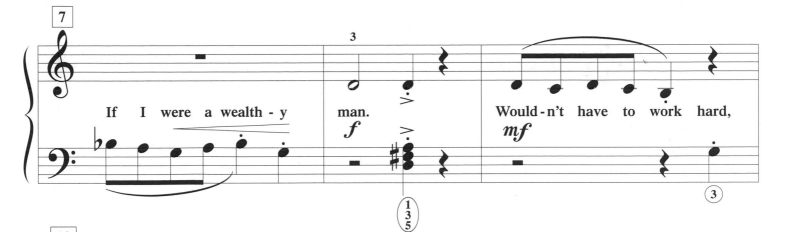

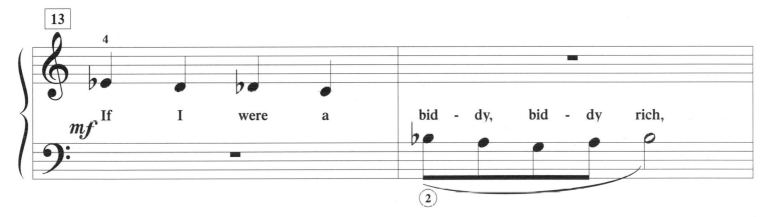

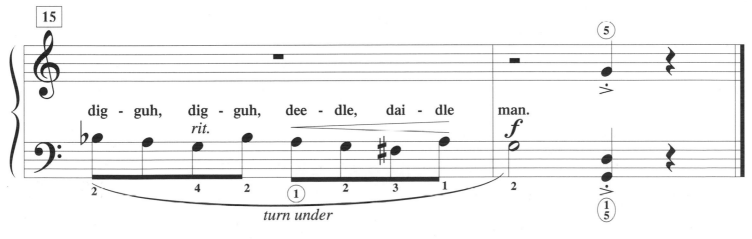

turn under

DISCOVERY Point out two measures that move down by *half steps*.
(For a review of half steps, see the Music Dictionary on pages 32–33.)

If I Were Transposing

Playing a melody in a different position is called **transposition**. The tune will be the same, but played at a higher or lower pitch.

Here is the opening melody of *If I Were a Rich Man* beginning on different notes. Notice the note names change, but the **intervals** stay the same.

Circle the starting position for the L.H.:

D Position, G Position, A Position

If I Were a Rich Man

Music by Jerry Bock

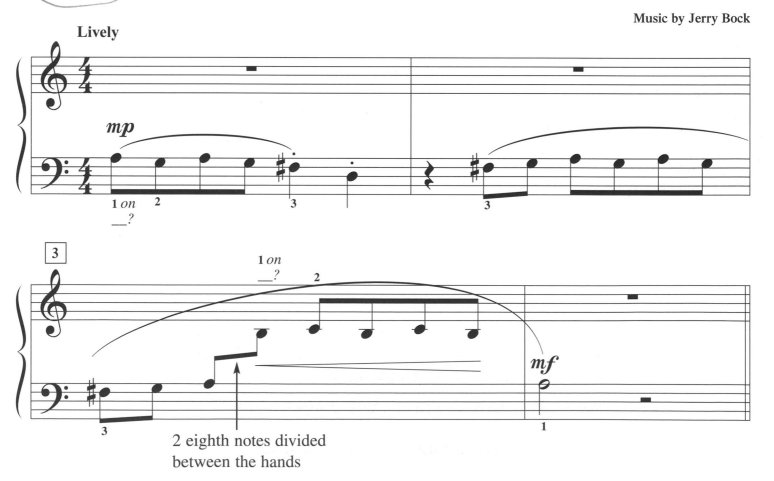

2 eighth notes divided
between the hands

FF1258

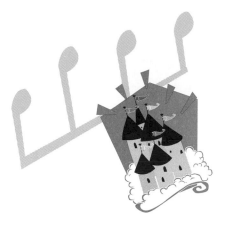

Circle the starting position for the L.H.:

D Position,   G Position,   **A Position**

If I Were a Rich Man

Music by Jerry Bock

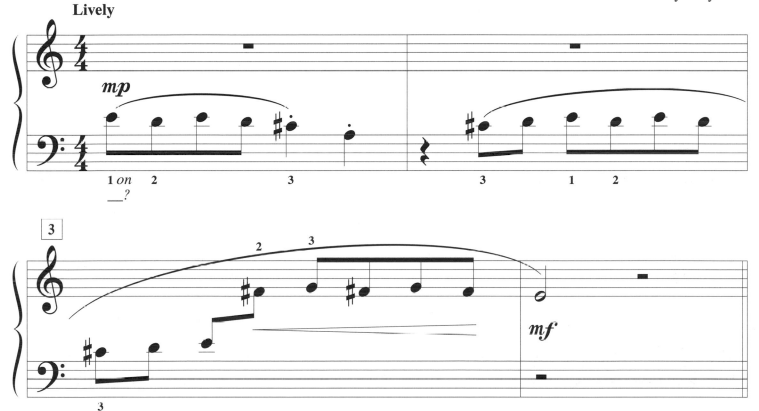

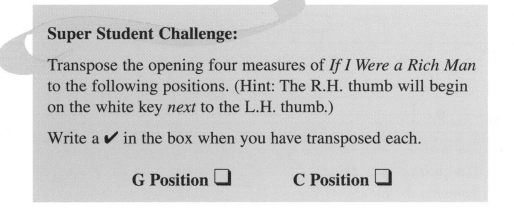

Super Student Challenge:

Transpose the opening four measures of *If I Were a Rich Man* to the following positions. (Hint: The R.H. thumb will begin on the white key *next* to the L.H. thumb.)

Write a ✔ in the box when you have transposed each.

G Position ☐   C Position ☐

A *phrase* is a musical idea or thought.
A phrase is often shown in the music with
a slur, also called a *phrase mark*.

phrase mark

keep Rythm!

Melody
Harmony
✗ Rhythm

The Merry Old Land of Oz

from *THE WIZARD OF OZ*

Lyric by E.Y. Harburg

Music by Harold Arlen

Moderately, with spirit

Ha - ha - ha! Ho - ho - ho! and (a) coup - le of tra - la -
'Bzz - 'bzz - 'bzz, Chirp, chirp, chirp, and (a) coup - le of la - de -

las, That's *phrase* how we laugh the day a - way, in the
das, That's how the crick - ets crick all day in the

Teacher Duet: (Student plays 1 octave higher)

R.H.

L.H.

p-mp on repeats

To Coda

mf

D.C. al Coda   Coda

mf

FF1258

DISCOVERY Point out the first *phrase mark*.
Point out where this phrase appears again in the music.

The Listening Land of Oz

Your teacher will play example **a** or **b**.
Listen and watch the notes carefully.
Also notice the *slurs* and *staccatos*.

• Then circle the example you hear.

1a.

or

1b.

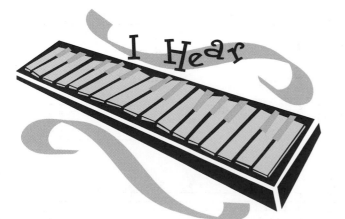

2a.

or

2b.

3a.

or

3b.

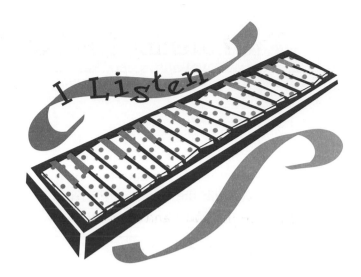

I Listen

4a.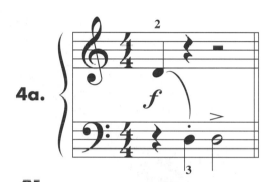

or

4b.

5a.

or

5b.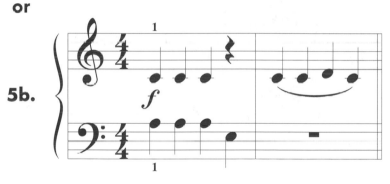

I Hear

6a.

or

6b.

Tempo marks

Allegro — fast and lively
Moderato — moderately, slower than *Allegro*
Andante — "walking speed," slower than *Moderato*

Tomorrow
from *ANNIE*

Lyric by
Martin Charnin

Music by
Charles Strouse

Teacher Duet: (Student plays 1 octave higher, without pedal)

FF1258

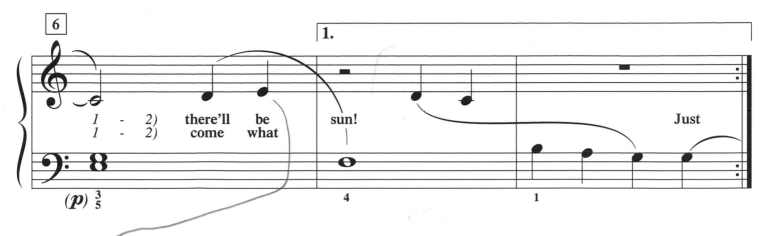

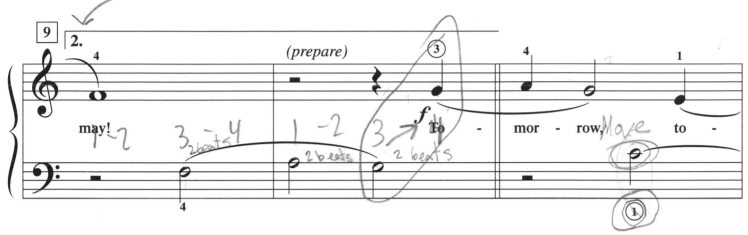

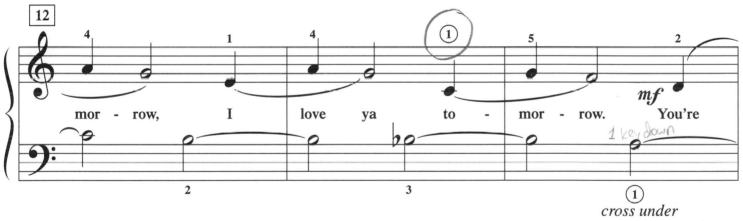

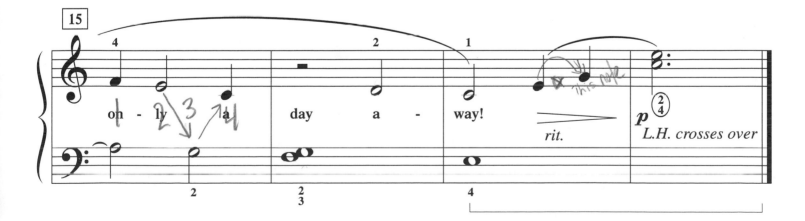

 DISCOVERY Tap (or clap) this rhythm for your teacher. ♩ ♩ ♩ ♩

Draw a star above each measure that uses this rhythm.

(Hint: There are five measures.)

You're Only a Bar Line Away!

Review of Rests

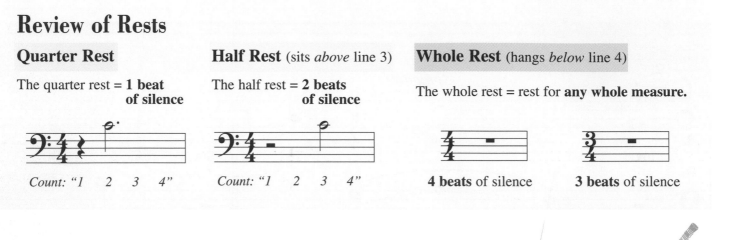

Quarter Rest

The quarter rest = **1 beat of silence**

Count: "1   2   3   4"

Half Rest (sits *above* line 3)

The half rest = **2 beats of silence**

Count: "1   2   3   4"

Whole Rest (hangs *below* line 4)

The whole rest = rest for **any whole measure.**

4 beats of silence   **3 beats** of silence

This music for *Tomorrow* is missing **bar lines** and **rests**.

- Notice the time signature. Then add bar lines.
- Draw a **quarter rest**, **half rest**, or **whole rest** to complete the measures. (The arrows will guide you.)

Tomorrow

**Music by
Charles Strouse**

FF1258

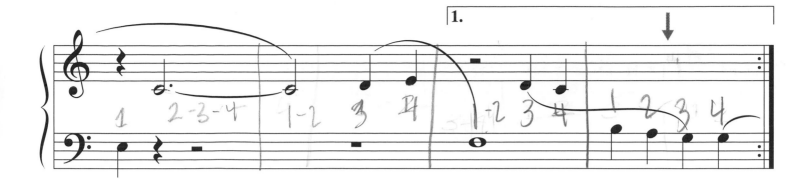

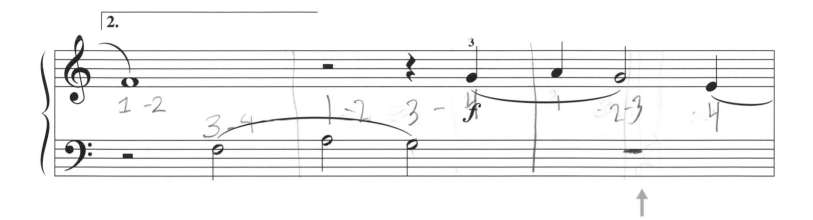

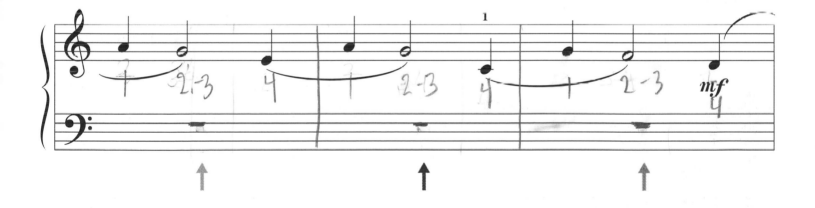

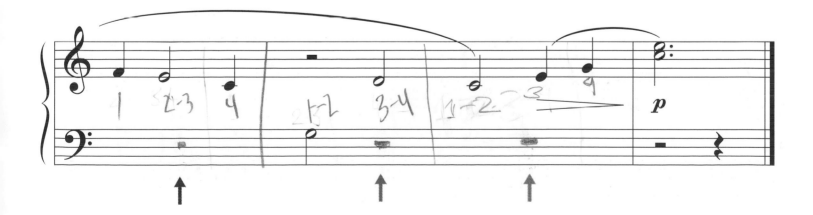

Splish, Splash

Words and Music by
Bobby Darin and Jean Murray

Allegro

Splish, splash, I was takin' a bath
Bing, splash, bang, move saw the whole bath gang

'long a-bout a Sat-ur-day night.
danc-in' on my liv-in' room rug.

Teacher Duet: (Student plays 1 octave higher)

FF1258

Musical Bubbles

Draw a connecting line to pair the bubbles that belong together.

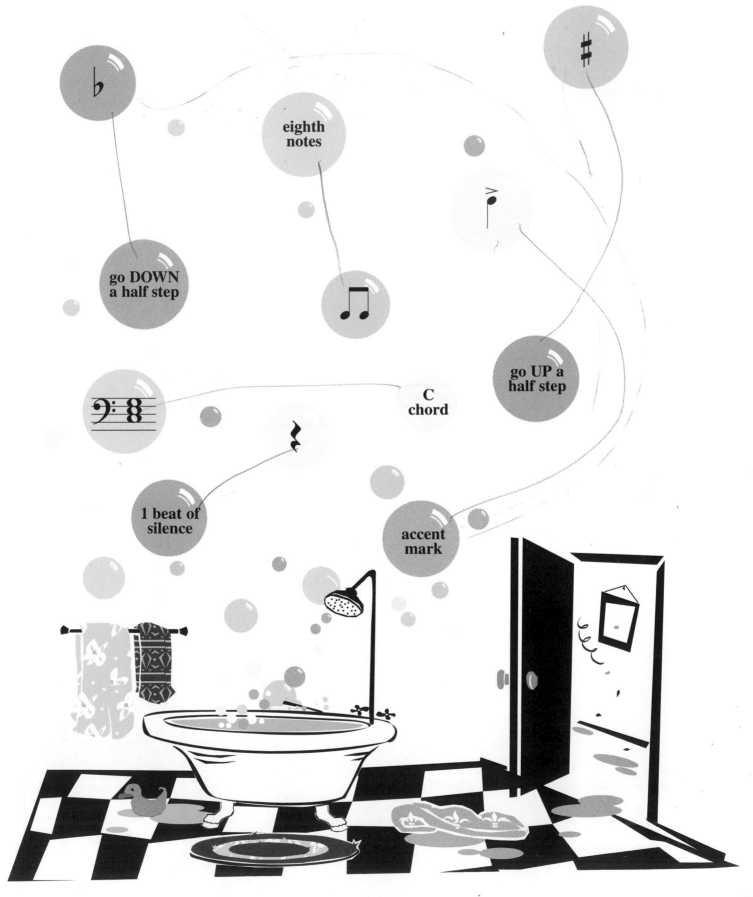

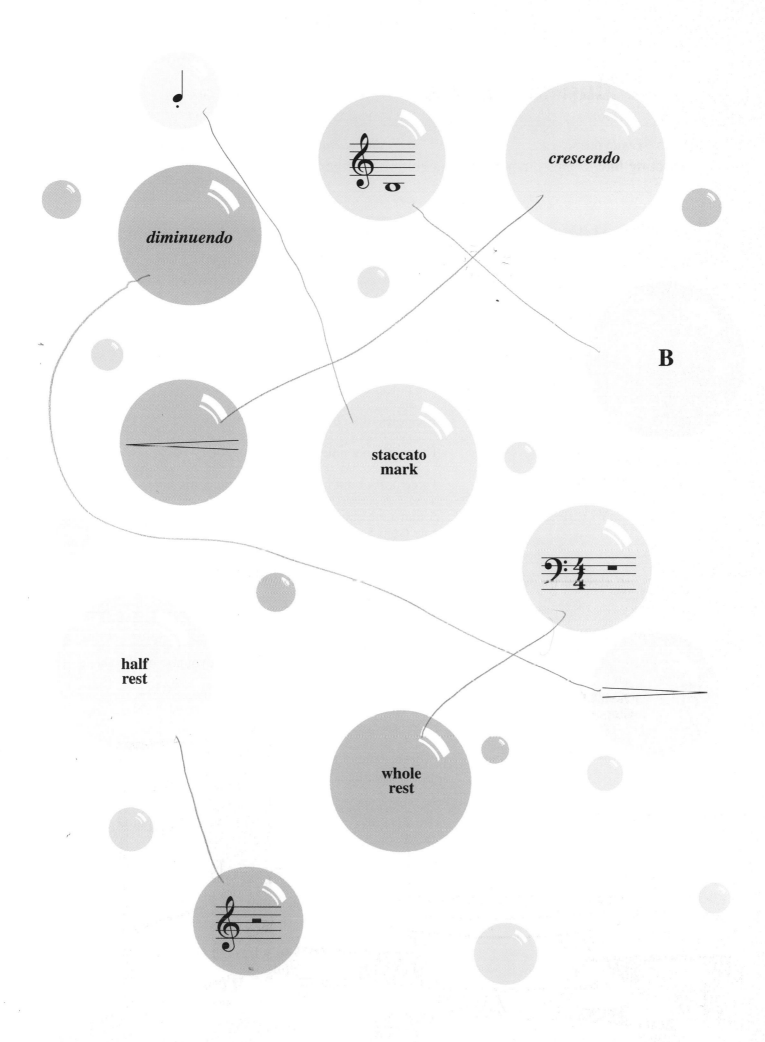

MUSIC DICTIONARY

p	mp	mf	f
piano	*mezzo piano*	*mezzo forte*	*forte*
soft	medium soft	medium loud	loud

crescendo (cresc.)
Play gradually louder.

diminuendo (dim.) or decrescendo (decresc.)
Play gradually softer.

SIGN	TERM	DEFINITION
	**accent mark**✱	Play this note louder.
	Allegro✱	Fast, lively tempo.
	Andante✱	Walking tempo.
	**bar line**✱	A line that divides the music into measures.
	**blocked chord**✱	The notes of a chord played together.
	**broken chord**✱	The notes of a chord played separately.
	chord✱	Three or more notes sounding together.
	I ("one") chord✱	Three notes built up in 3rds from the tonic note.
	V7 ("five-seven")✱	A four-note chord built up in 3rds from the dominant note (step 5 of the scale), often played with only two or three notes.
	damper pedal✱	The pedal on the right. It lifts the dampers off the strings, allowing the sound to continue to ring.
C 5-note scale 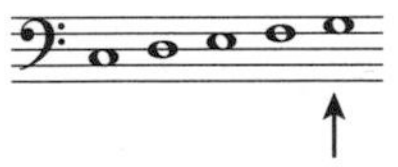	**dominant**✱	The fifth note of the scale.
	dynamics✱	The "louds and softs" of music. See dynamic marks above.
	**eighth notes**✱	Two eighth notes equal one quarter note.
	fermata✱	Hold this note longer than its usual value.
 1. 2.	**1st and 2nd endings**✱	Play the 1st ending and take the repeat. Then play the 2nd ending, skipping over the 1st ending.
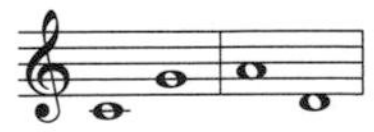	**fifth (5th)**	The interval of a 5th spans five letter names. (Ex. C up to G, or A down to D) Line-(skip-a-line)-line, or space-(skip-a-space)-space.
 ♭	**flat**	A flat lowers a note one half step.
	**fourth (4th)**	The interval of a 4th spans four letter names. (Ex. C up to F, or A down to E) Line-(skip-a-line)-space. or space-(skip-a-space)-line.
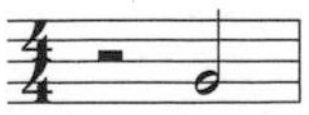	**half rest**	Silence for two counts or beats.
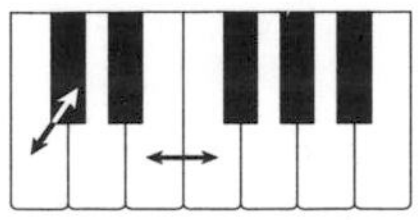	**half step**	The distance from one key to the very closest key on the keyboard. (Ex. C-C♯ or E-F)
	interval	The distance between two musical tones or keys on the keyboard.

(handwritten annotations:) FINISHED · 27 · accent mark - louder · ♭ lowers a note ½ half step

FF1258